RÉSUMÉ

RESUMÉ

PRACTICE BOOK FOR THE
TWELVE LESSONS
IN HIGH MYSTICISM

first set forth in 1892

by

EMMA CURTIS HOPKINS

WiseWoman Press

Resumé: Practice book for the twelve lessons in high mysticism
By Emma Curtis Hopkins

Published By WiseWoman Press, Beaverton, Oregon: 2007

Based on the text published by Sanctuary Of Truth, Alhambra, California, 1996

Managing Editor: Michael Terranova
Design: Ruth Miller

ISBN: 978-0-945385-11-0

NOTA BENE

"He that would perfect himself in any art whatsoever, let him betake himself to the reading of some sure and certain work upon his art many times over; for to read many books upon your art produceth confusion rather than learning." ~ Old Saying.

"*Cave ab hominem unius libri...*" (Beware the man of one book - he knows) ~ Roman Proverb.

"Yea, even a single person occupying with the Thora is sure of reward." ~ *Thora*.

"And a book of remembrance was written." ~ *Malachi 3:16*.

"Seek ye out of the book of the Lord, and read: no one of these shall fail." ~ *Isaiah 3:16*.

"And I wept much because no man was found worthy (willing to persist) to open and to read the book." ~ *Revelation 5:4*.

CONTENTS

TO REMEMBER:

Commit to memory this page of Bible texts on the first Study:

"The Lord looketh upon all the inhabitants of the earth." ~ *Psalm 33:14*

"Look unto me and be ye saved, all the ends of the earth, for I am God and there is none *else.* " ~ *Isaiah 45:22.*

"Repent and turn away your faces from all your abominations." ~ *Ezekiel 14:6.*

"Behold, he cometh with clouds, and every eye shall see him."~ *Revelation 1:7.*

"They sing the song of Moses, and the song of the Lamb." ~ *Revelation 15:3.*

"That led them by the right hand of Moses with his glorious arm, dividing the waters before them, to make himself an everlasting name." ~ *Isaiah 63:12.*

"That repentance should be preached in his name, beginning at Jerusalem." ~ *Luke 24:47.*

I

REPENTANCE[1]

The High and Lofty One inhabiting Eternity has been understood by His lovers to be forever inviting mankind to look unto His Countenance shining as the sun with healing strength.

The Deity looketh upon us; let us look to the Deity. This is the way of salvation from sin, sickness, misfortune and death.

Isaiah understood it as a Soundless Mandate: "Look unto me and be ye saved, all the ends of the earth" *(Is. 45:22)*. Ezekiel understood it as the law of repentance, or returning: "Repent, and turn away your faces from all your abominations" *(Ezek. 14:6)*. Jesus called it The Watch: "What I say unto you, I say unto all, Watch" *(Mark 13:37)*. Plato understood the Watch as a privilege: "It is time to lift the eye of the soul above the outlandish slough in which it is buried, and set it toward the Elysian Fields."

---

[1] This is Monday morning's study.

1

It has been found that what we vision steadily causes our thinking. Even Hegel noticed this law in his *Introduction to Logic*, where he avers that we secretly perceive toward an object before thinking it.

If we exhibit in this posit we call our "me" according to the direction we oftenest set this visional sense, which can see toward God or toward the workings of our own brain, it is high time we set the important and all-achieving sense definitely toward that objective calculated to build us to the best advantage.

If back over the Tao, or Track, of this wonderful sense can come infinitesimal pictures of the objective it views toward, we will choose the "Great, the Mighty God, great in counsel and mighty in work" *(Jer. 32:19)*, for our objective. This is the way of being God-taught. "I will instruct thee and teach thee" *(Ps. 32:8)*. It is the way of being divinely guided. "I will guide thee with mine eye" *(Ps. 32:8)*.

John the Revelator was God-taught. He saw all truth in symbols, or pictures. He called the great lessons he learned, "Angels," or messages. He divided them into seven. The seventh he repeats over and over, like Joshua sounding one tone with rams' horns on the seventh day of his circling of Jericho. The tone John sounds is, "I looked, " and, "I beheld."

With obedience to the mandate, "Look unto me," John saw hail and fire mingled with blood falling upon the earth (*Rev. 8*). "Hail" is new fresh truth. How can we help having new truth if we set our eye in a new direction? It is the resistless truth of the eternal Heights. "Fire" is the emblem of heavenly fervor. The heart flames up with new zeal, new ardor, new love, if the vision is upward.

"Blood" is the emblem of new life. Men can appear who were not born of the will of man but of the will of God. Such an one walked along with Tobias. Such an one appeared to Jacob. Such an one sometimes appears in our own age. Two were seen by a highway robber to be walking along with a missionary at midnight when the missionary supposed himself to be alone. The robber hurried away from the three of them.

This is the new life we cannot help encountering as we seek our highest Good at the highest Source. The disciples felt their hearts burn while such an one talked with them as they walked toward Emmaus. Their oftime gaze had been heavenward where on the right hand of God Omnipotent they had visioned their Lord and Master, Jesus the Christ.

As a result of their upward watch, the empowering Angel of God's presence was tangible to them. Such appearances are the blood of obedience.

John the Revelator sees a third of the trees disappear. He sees all the green grass burn up *(Rev. 8)*. "Trees" are the emblems of flourishing practices. One third of these practices cease, even in the life of the individual, as the flaming zeal for God kindles.

Competitive examinations competitive trades, competitive platforms, which constitute the ginger and glow of unvisioning life, cease for such as know that their true provisions and their true positions come straight from above, and nothing and nobody can take them from them.

All strenuousness on every line must cease. The laborers and anarchists, the pole hunters and the gold grabbers must calm down, for the Countenance that shineth hot with healing tenderness and rich giving is of more value than all that can possibly come by the clash of endeavor.

"Grass" is emblem of the seasons of human life, childhood, youth, middle age, old age, such as the new people know not. Did the Son of God, seen in the fiery furnace by the King of Babylon, know anything of childhood and old age? *(Dan. 3)*. The upward watch of the King must once have been true and steady to have found in the fiery furnace the man with eternity stamped upon his brow. The robber who beheld the two guardsmen of the missionary must have at some moment of his life looked upward, whence the daysprings fall, and some of the prisons where he was shut in must have sometimes been unaccountably opened for him. For the High and Lofty Majesty inhabiting Eternity is the "bad man's deliverer," said Lao-tze the God-taught.

The visional sense that seeks the Vast Countenance ever shining hitherward, can bring back news of any objective it sets itself toward, from the rocks of the gorges to the midnight stars. Did not untaught Bramahaupto find out the names and the motions of the suns and constellations by gazing toward them even in his dreams? Can you not feel that a starry radiance must have shone forth from Bramahaupto's eyes, since, "that thou seest man that too become thou must?"

Obeying the sublime mandate, "Look unto me," we sense the mystery of redemptive energy. John tells us that the Redeemed are given two songs *(Rev. 15)*. Perpetually recurring names are songs. Job was the song of his scornful neighbors. *"I AM that I AM"* was the song of Moses. *"Jesus Christ"* was the song of the first Christians. These names are full of the meaning of life and the transports of Eternal Truth.

Zoroaster was told that the name *"I AM that I AM"* is the name of kingly might and majesty. He repeated it often and stepped out of the rank and file of men into rulership of the nation.

"The Lord is high above all nations and his glory above the heavens.

"Who is like unto the Lord our God who

exalteth himself to dwell on high?

"He raiseth the poor up out of the dust that He may set him with princes" *(Ps. 113).*

With that Name, which means that no one knows the nature and character of Him that bears it, Moses led two million slaves to triumphant liberty: "That led them by the right hand of Moses with his glorious arm, dividing the waters before them, to make himself an everlasting name" *(Is. 63).*

With the Song of the Lamb in his heart, Peter converted three thousand people to Christianity by one transcendent sermon. "There is none other name under heaven given among men, whereby we must be saved," he said *(Acts 4:12).*

Let us take Monday to repent, or turn away our faces from all the things, events and people that call our attention. Let us often look upward toward the Deity ever beholding us. Let us tell that "*Ain Soph*, Great Countenance of the Absolute above thinking and above being," as the Kabala avers, that we know His Name of up lifting might; His Name of majesty and grandeur. It is *I AM that I AM.* Let us tell Him that we know His Name of manifestation in the flesh; His embodying Name, His Name of our own manifested health and undefeatable free Spirit. It is *Jesus Christ.*

It is on the principle of doing things in order, as Paul enjoined. *(1 Cor. 14:40),* that we begin the week days with obedience to the heavenly ordinance, "Look unto Me," which is preaching repentance, beginning at Jerusalem, or the Self *(Luke 24:47)*.

TO REMEMBER:

Commit to memory this page of Bible texts on the second Study:

"That remission should be preached in all nations beginning at Jerusalem." ~ *Luke 24:47.*

"Then Peter said unto them, Repent, and be baptized every one of you in the name of Jesus Christ for the remission of sins, and ye shall receive the gift of the Holy Ghost." ~ *Acts 2:38.*

"Looking diligently lest any man fail of the grace of *God.*" ~ *Hebrews 12:15.*

"Nothing shall by any means hurt you." ~ *Luke 10:19.*

"Thou dissolvest my substance." ~ *Job 30:22.*

"The earth and all the inhabitants thereof are dissolved." ~ *Psalms 75:3.*

"If any man will come after me, let him deny himself." ~ *Matthew 16:24.*

II

REMISSION[2] _Liberation_

On the Principle that what we oftenest view with the inner eye, that we show forth outwardly, we can easily understand why the poor cripple near the temple gate *(Acts 3)*, with vision in the dust, had never felt the dissolving of the manacles of impotence till Peter and John bade him look up.

Something then fell down over his upward visioning and undid his chains of mind and body. "Preach remission," said Jesus. "Preach the dissolving Grace."

"When men are cast down thou shalt say, 'There is lifting up,' and God shall save the humble person," said Eliphaz *(Job 22:29)*. There are shouts of freedom handed down from antiquity that represent the experiences of remission, or liberation of the upward watchers throughout the ages. They declare the disappearings of foolishness and ignorance. They are recognitions that foolish virgins or objectives, with no oil of healing

---

[2] This is Tuesday morning's study.

9

and no oil of illuminating in their sayings, are shut out.

There is no oil of healing and no oil of illuminating in descriptions of evil in any way. Description of evil is a foolish virgin. The description of evil doubles evil. It does not lessen it. See then how foolish to describe evil and thereby double it. If we see an army of locusts alighting on the green vegetation we mourn because the people must starve. This is our foolishness. We increase starvation by such mourning. According to Jesus the risen and triumphant man of God, we are to look up to the shining face of our Father looking tenderly down upon us, and declare, "Steadfastly facing Thee, there is no evil on my pathway." For only abundance and gentle kindness fall from the Vast Countenance shining hitherward.

According to the experiences of the men of light, the locusts must vanish in all directions if we exalt our vision above them—dissolved like the Ammonites, Moabites, and Seirs, from Jehoshaphat's pathway, when he said, "Oh, our God, our eyes are upon Thee" (2 *Chron. 20*).

St. Augustine found that God sees no evil. So also did Habakkuk *(1:13)*. We catch the viewpoint of those with whom we associate. Let us catch the High God's viewpoint and go free from sight of evil. Zephaniah cried, "Shout, O Zion: thou shalt not see evil any more!" *(Zeph. 8)*. He saw for a short period as his God was seeing.

Matter also has been found to have no health in its operations. No descriptions of matter quicken the pulses with healing blood, or fill the stomach with strengthening energy. No study of matter illuminates the spiritual wisdoms that wait like unlighted candles just above our heads. Only the kindling fires of God's hot glance can illuminate our waiting intelligence. And we must recognize the glance, acting under obedience to the order, "Behold Me" *(Is. 65)*.

Matter moves aside for indestructible free grace to act, when by upward viewing we shout, "Facing Thee, there is no matter with its laws."

Neither is there any oil of healing in descriptions of lack and deprivation. This is the foolish virgin that woman is said to hug to herself. "No wine," she says. "Not enough — not enough of this, or of that good thing." She must let go that foolish saying, and look up to him who saith, "They shall want for no good thing" *(Ps. 34:10)*. She must preach to the heavens that facing the Father there is neither lack nor deprivation.

There is no acting free grace visible to one who describes hurts and pains. Peter sank into the raging waters when he took his gaze off the powerful Jesus *(Matt. 14)*. But with his eye uplifted he walked above the waves, side by side with Omnipotence. There is a shout of liberty anyone can give when hurts come grinding and burning upon him: "Facing Thee, there is nothing to fear, for nothing shall by any means hurt me" *(Luke 10:19)*. All hurting power is darkness. The dayspring from on high gives light to them that sit in darkness, to guide their feet into the way of peace *(Luke 1:79)*.

Sinfulness with its sickness and death is only the description of what is encountered by men with aberrated vision, or downward gaze. It is downward gazing to describe a child's bad temper or a friend's unkindness. Not only they, but we who describe, must get warped and ill by reason of the excitement their ill behavior causes us. It is the one foolish virgin that works with surprising haste. See how quickly you have cramps, or influenza, or something else, when you are excited by the willfulness or deception of your wife, or husband, or friend.

The shout of the free must be given before we feel the freedom, as the Sons of Judah at the watchtower in the wilderness shouted liberty before they came into it *(2 Chron. 20)*. Did not Jesus shout, "It is finished," before it was finished? But see how quickly the anguish left him when he shouted with a loud voice, "It is finished" *(John 19:30)*.

Let us take Tuesday to shout liberty, free grace — remission — unburdening, as we look upward. Free grace comes softly stealing over the Tao, or Track, of the upward watch. Take the shouts in order. Look up to the Vast Countenance with its beaming and kindling free grace, its dissolving alkahest, ever hitherward streaming, and with joyous heart proclaim:

Facing Thee, there is no evil on my pathway;

There is no matter with its laws;

There is no loss, no lack, no deprivation;

There is nothing to fear for there shall be no power to hurt;

There is neither sin, nor sickness, nor death.

Because Thou Art The Unconditioned and The Absolute, I also am Unconditioned and Absolute.

Because Thou Art Omnipotent Free Spirit, I also am Omnipotent Free Spirit.

TO REMEMBER:

Commit to memory this page of Bible texts on the third Study:

"There is forgiveness with Thee." ~ *Psalm 130:4.*

"To the Lord our God belong forgivenesses." ~ *Daniel 9:9.*

"If my people, upon whom my name is called, shall humble themselves, and seek my face, and turn from their wicked ways; then will I hear from heaven, and will forgive all their land." ~ *2 Chronicles 7:14.*

"He that humbleth himself shall be exalted." ~ *Luke 14:11.*

"Put on humbleness of mind, and meekness." ~ *Colossians 3:12.*

"Because thine heart was tender, and thou didst humble thyself before God — I have even heard thee also, saith the Lord " ~ *2 Chronicles 34:27.*

"Behold, my servant shall prosper, he shall be exalted and extolled, and be very high." ~ *Isaiah 52:13.*

"Who forgiveth all thine iniquities, who healeth all thy diseases." ~ *Psalm 103:3.*

III

FORGIVENESS[3]

If nothing hurts Free Spirit and I am Free Spirit, unhurt forever, I have something given *for* the imagination of hurting which has now slipped away from me. This that takes the place of hurts is Beauty, Joy, Praise, Wholeness. The Hindus stay enchained in devotion to removals, dissolvings, non-estness. They bury themselves in the ground to show that nothing can by any means hurt them. They transform material things out of sight by denial of materiality. They call the body the dark shadow of the Soul. They teach to regard the body as of no concern to the True Self. "To know this disregard as righteousness is true liberation, the highest state the sage can attain" (*Zend-Avesta*, Fluegel's translation, p. 94). The Hebrews touch lightly upon what disappears. They describe with flourishing of banners the splendors seen when the shadows pass: "My servant shall be exalted, he shall deal prudently, and be very high" (*Is. 52*).

---

[3] This is Wednesday morning's study.

"The Lord God hath given me the tongue of the learned" *(Is. 50)*. It was Hebrew before it was Christian to preach forgiveness, or the given-for; as: "the garment of praise for the spirit of heaviness;" and "the plantings that glorify God, *for* desolation" *(Is: 61)*. "The Lord shall forgive" *(Num. 30)*.

As the needle can become a magnet by rubbing against a magnet, so we can do God-works by closely relating ourselves to the Healer of all diseases, the Redeemer from destruction, the Great in Counsel. As the needle must utterly yield herself so must we utterly yield our selves. We must have our eye single to One Only to be full of that One Only. Utter yielding is called "meekness," in the Scriptures.

There is a Divine Fiat ever going forth. There is a Divine Providence always acting. If we hold the magnetic needle still it is restless till it is free to point north. So we are restless under the cramps formulated by our own visioning toward evil, or the body of matter, of pain and decay. These slough off with the high watch and the shouts of the free. We sense the Divine Providence — the Heavenly Fiat. The sense of the kind and good and joy-giving Providence upbearing us forever, has been called the "Cosmic Consciousness." Its ecstasy of rest in the Lord has been called "forgiveness."

Great Proclamations have issued forth from those who have experienced the cosmic con-

a command or act that creates something without fut further effort sciousness, or forgiveness. These proclamations have been called "Affirmations of Eternal Truth." They have been called "Hymns to the Eternal." They have been figuratively spoken of as "Wise Virgins," with oil of healing and oil of illuminating in their influence. As the needle cannot attract like a magnet if it does not yield itself *in toto* to the magnet, so no man can be the embodiment of the five eternal proclamations who has not let his mind, his life, his heart, his body go free to the winds of the Divine Fiat, looking up often to the Sun of Righteousness with healing in his wings.

Professor William James tells of an Oxford graduate who volitionally offered himself to the Stream of Divine Order, letting go of himself like a reed in the wind, fully expecting annihilation. To his surprise he found his bad habits gone, his despair dissolved, his character and body strengthened and his whole being infused with radiance. Hannah let herself go into the Divine Order, through self-abnegating prayer, till she staggered. Eli the prophet thought she was drunken with wine. But she was like the needle just ready to rise into powerful repute. Suddenly, Eli prophesies for her, and she shouts the gist of the five great affirmations of truth:

> "There is none beside Thee. The Lord shall judge the ends of the earth; and he shall give strength unto the king, and exalt the horn of his Anointed" (*I Sam. 2*).

The risen Christ taught volitional meekness, volitional offering: "He that humbleth himself shall be exalted" *(Luke 14:11).*

Let us take Wednesday to voluntarily offer our self to the King of Kings and Lord of Lords. They that worship in meekness are the ready harp strings for the divine melodies of the five hymns of praise, the five proclamations of truth. They are the voicing instruments of Health and quickening life.

Here is a form for voluntary surrender of self in meekness, and the, full text of all the illuminative sayings for centuries, whenever men have found themselves yielding in humility and rising up for given:

Here is my mind. I spread it out before Thee. Forgive Thou its foolishness and ignorance with Thy bright wisdom. Here is my life. I offer it to Thee. Forgive Thou its contrariness to Thee. Here is my heart. It is Thine only. Forgive Thou its restlessness and dissatisfaction. Forgive its discouragements. Forgive its resentments. Forgive its loves and its hates, its hopes and its fears. Here is my body. I cast it down before Thee. Forgive Thou its imperfection with Thy perfection. Forgive me altogether with Thyself. Give for myself Thyself. So only can I know that:

Thou art, and there is none beside Thee, in Thine own Omnipresence, Omnipotence, Omniscience—

I am Thine only and in Thee I live, move, and

have being—

I am Thine own substance, power, and light, and I shed abroad wisdom, strength, holiness, from Thee—

Thou art now working through me to will and to do that which ought to be done by me—

I am forgiven and governed by Thee alone, and I cannot sin, I cannot suffer for sin, nor fear sin, sickness or death.

"Bow down thyself to me and thou shalt come even to me. Take sanctuary with me alone and I shall liberate thee from all sin, by the resplendent Lamp of Wisdom" (*Vedic Hymn*).

With the experience of forgiveness, or the *Hestia Vestia* of bold Truth, John foresees a star called, "Wormwood," falling to the earth *(Rev. 8:10)*. A "star" is a great character. And "wormwood" is mind preserver, or mind cure. One shall be the embodiment of Truth so inspiringly that he shall cure the world mind of its earth-drowse.

When a man is sick or in pain, he is in telluric slumber or earth-drowse. He is magnetized by foolishness and ignorance. His mind is thralled by foolishness and ignorance: the earth-sleep. John the Revelator sees one to arise all awake. His vivid sense of Living Spirit shall kindle in men now asleep the vivid sense of Living Spirit, of the giving for matter's laws the law of the Spirit of life in Christ Jesus.

TO REMEMBER:

Commit to memory this page of Bible texts on the fourth Study:

"Let us therefore come boldly unto the throne of grace." ~ *Hebrews 4:16.*

"Faith is the confidence of things hoped for." ~ *Hebrews 11:1.*

"In whom we have boldness and access with confidence by the faith of him." ~ *Ephesians 3:12.*

"The revelation of the mystery, which was kept secret since the world began, but now is made manifest, according to the commandment of the everlasting God — for the obedience of faith." ~ *Romans 16:25, 26.*

"Concerning the work of my hands command ye me." ~ *Isaiah 45:11.*

"Here are they that keep the commandments of God and the faith of Jesus." ~ *Revelation 14:12.*

IV

FAITH[4]

That nature rises up in us before which we have worshipped. The meek Jesus was worshipper before the King of Kings and Lord of Lords, therefore he must at some moment proclaim. "All power is given unto me in heaven and in earth" *(Matt 28:18).* "I have overcome the world" *(John 16:83).* "He that hath seen me hath seen the father" *(John 14:9).*

Napoleon was meek before the generals of the French army and rose up head of the army. Joan of Arc was meek before the angels who had accompanied her all her life, and she rose up with supernatural powers, Both Napoleon and Joan of Arc fell, because there is no nature worth practicing subservience unto except the Ruler in the heavens and the earth, "Let the Lord be thy confidence, he will not suffer thy foot to be taken" *(Prov. 3:26)* "Hast thou faith? Have it to thyself before God" *(Rom. 14:22).*

God is the Author of faith, as Paul wrote to the Ephesians *(3:12),* which Jesus of Nazareth caught

---

[4] This is Thursday morning's study.

so completely that the whole creation was subject to his strong word of authority. Faith is always associated with authority. Faith is confidence to command. One little spark of it no larger than a mustard seed, would cause authority enough to move a mountain *(Matt 17:20)*, Moses caused two million people to obey his lightest command after the spark of authority flamed up in him. He had been meek and lowly to the loss of his self-consciousness, while kneeling before God on the mountains of Midian. Self-consciousness is a poor stuff to present before men or nature if we want to command them even for their good. Is if not Self-consciousness that makes a person appear poorly before his neighbors? It is the wiping out of this tough integument that lowliness before The King of Kings accomplishes. Self-consciousness is sometimes called self-will because it is a perversity of the whole constitution, and because the divine authority that rises out of its demolition is a new will.

Elisha had all his life been lowly before God. He bathed the hands and feet of Elijah while yet his eyes were heavenward. Suddenly, no man in Israel had so much authority over men and nature as the hitherto meek Elisha,

The exercise of authority is good exercise. It gets its kindling from practicing upon the most obedient servant first. The Supreme God is the most docile and obedient Servant. David commanded the High God: "Show me a token for good that they which hate me may see it" *(Ps. 86)* He was astonished at the results of his firm authority: "Thou through thy commandments hast made me wiser than mine enemies" *(Ps. 119)*,

Isaiah understood that we must practice commanding the Supreme Presence in the Universe. While listening in lowly humility before Him he heard these words, "Concerning the work of my hands command ye me" *(Is. 45)*.

Jesus commanded the Supreme Servant, "Glorify Thou me." On the cross he cried, "How Thou hast glorified me!" This is one of two translations of the words reported in *Mark 14* as "Why hast Thou forsaken me?" Jacob commanded the angel of God's presence, whom he called God himself, "I will not let thee go except thou bless me" *(Gen. 32:26)*. Job said, "I will demand of thee, and declare thou unto me" *(Job 42)*. Jesus commanded the God of Lazarus, He commanded the God of the withered arm. Always lowly meekness rises to confidence to command. Napoleon could never really understand how he came by such commanding confidence, but we can see that it was by reason of his prompt obedience to the authority he recognized vested in his superior officers.

Jesus told his disciples to speak to the Supreme Servant in the terms of the Lord's Prayer as the firm insistence of their own lordship or hidden man of the heart whom all authorities obey. It is a formula full of short commands to the Great Servant who asks, "Is anything too hard for me?" *(Jer. 32:27).*

We will take Thursday to practice speaking to the Great Servant with firm command, in the words of the hidden Lord's Formula. We will speak it over and over fifteen times, as the sick people do at the Waters of Lourdes when they are urging God to heal them by way of the Waters, "Fifteen" is the number where the waters of misfortune cease to prevail against us, as *Gen, 7:20,* It is the number of using to walk above hardship.

Notice that Marcella of the Roman Catholic Church, taught her nuns the inner meaning of "Give us this day our daily bread." She said it ought to be, "Give me this day my super-substantial bread." Our secret ego, our God-spark, our "hidden man of the heart," as Peter called it *(1 Peter 3:4),* must have the bread of heaven.

Notice how "Lead us not into temptation" has lately been translated as. "Let us not into temptation," or, "Let me not into temptation," meaning, "Warn me when I turn away from Thee." Notice how "Forgive us our debts" is now understood to be, "Give for our emptiness Thy Substance." Paul called faith a substance. There is a great mystery about "faith" which, as Paul's word "substance", is rendered as "confidence," in the margin of Hebrews eleventh chapter, first verse: "Faith is the confidence of things hoped for."

Grow more and more urgent, insistent, commanding, as you go on repeating the Great Formula to the Greatest Servant amongst us. Let confidence solidify. Let the God-spark speak. "The gods love courage armed with confidence" (*Bonduca*, translated by Beaumont and Fletcher).

TO REMEMBER:

Commit to memory this page of Bible texts on the fifth Study:

"And the word was made flesh, and dwelt among us, (and we beheld his glory, the glory as of the only begotten of the Father,) full of grace and truth." ~ *John 1:14.*

"Behold, my sheaf stood upright." ~ *Genesis 37:7.*

"He that ruleth his spirit is better than he that taketh a city." ~ *Proverbs 16:32.*

"Pleasant words are sweet to the soul." ~ *Proverbs 16:24.*

"When thou shalt make his soul an offering..." ~ *Isaiah 53:10.*

"I have finished the work Thou gavest me to do." ~ *John 17:4.*

"As far is the east is from the west, so far hath he removed our transgressions from us." ~ *Psalm 103:12.*

"That he might deliver us from this present evil world..." ~ *Galatians 1:4.*

V

WORKS[5]

Faith without works does not exist. Faith always works. It stirs boldness, confidence, to dare the seemingly impossible. Notice Elisha's bold faith when he ordered the widow to borrow vessels and pour oil, seemingly from nowhere, into them (2 *Kings* 4). Command of the Great Servant is a practice that changes the nature from timidity and doubt to commanding boldness, from timid following to daring leadership, from obedience to authority. So was Jacob's name changed to "Israel" when he fought with the angel till daybreak, and won in the battle (*Gen. 32*).

Authority with God discloses authority with the Self. The divine Self, the *esse*, lies quiescent, still, waiting in all men to be stirred into action by the outer self. Two kinds of address stir the still *esse* to action, viz., command and praise.

Solomon lauded the ruling of the Spirit (*Prov.* 16:32). Recognize the Spirit and it acts. Recogni-

---

[5] This is Friday morning's study.

tion has a subtle law of its own. Body, and its speech are woven into relationship with the Soul, or Self, or *esse*, by recognition. Walt Whitman said, "I believe in you, my Soul." He said, "Loose the throttle of my throat." So did Isaiah say, "Loose thy self from the bands of thy neck, O captive daughter of Zion!" *(Is. 52).*

The Hindus explain this for us by telling us to turn and speak to the divine Self back of us. As our speech has hitherto been all shot forward, speaking to our neighbor, so now at the turn of the tongue, we speak backward to upraise our outer self by our hidden Self. This Self back of us, like a Shekinah pillar of cloud by day and of fire by night, is the friend of our outer self, or outer life. It can make the outer life whole and strong, and sane.

Man is not really sane while his body is ill. For he that is truly sane knows the health he can waken outwardly by recognizing his Soul's free, flawless, immortal excellence. "The Spirit of a man is the candle of the Lord", said Solomon *(Prov. 20:27).* And by recognizing this candle sound health is established in the outer man. "Awake up, my glory!" shouted David *(Ps. 57:8).* "Awake thou that sleepest!" cried Paul *(Eph. 5:14).* They are addressing, with strong command, the ever-present glorious Soul. And both David and Paul thereby awoke divine chords of being in themselves for all ages to wonder at.

awaken my divine chords of being my limitless self the instill in me boldness and confidence of they Spirit

He whose Soul glows and flames through all he does and thinks, has discovered a bottomless well of living refreshment to draw from. Everything he does has the touch of spiritual charm about it. For the Soul is the everlasting reservoir of enchantment. "The fifth angel sounded," said John the Revelator *(Rev. 9)*, and a star-like character appeared upon the earth, teaching men to draw from the depths of their own Soul, or the bottomless well of power and glory. And John saw that the man of Soul showed men how to put their consciousness of flesh limitation and common sensations of pain and pleasure into trance, or sleep, for the sense of God's presence to be most real. And thereby should men know new laws of life, having in them as much strength as the scorpion law of labor, law of lucre, law of learning, law of loving have strength. This is the stone of the New Law that filled all the earth in Daniel's vision *(Dan. 2)*.

For centuries on centuries we have been urged by Hebrew and Hindu to praise and command the hidden limitless Self of us. Let us begin now, this night, to praise and command the Self: "Oh, Wonderful Me! Oh, strong and unspoilable Me! Beautiful Me! Influential Me, Enchanting and Immortal Wisdom!" It answers, "I am all that and more." For "It hath not entered into the heart of man to conceive," said Paul *(I Cor. 2)*, what is in the storehouse laid up.

Let us continue with strong commands to our great Self: Rise up, my Soul, and heal the sick wherever I walk! Show people how to be strong! Make people love God! Quicken me with heavenly fervor! Show me the finished kingdom through which I walk! Show me the words that make the world glad and sane!

The Soul, or Free Spirit, answers, "I can all that and more." We must never give over commanding the Soul Self every night of the life before we sleep. Some day, like Jesus of Nazareth, we shall sense our ever-present abilities. It was by the sense of his masterful Soul that he saw he could take all the sin and all the consequences of the sins of the world, into himself, and because he was full of the Godhead bodily, he could utterly annihilate sin, sickness and death.

There is a strange and very little observed law ever operative among us. It is the law of vicarious or transferred suffering. Jesus saw this law and entered into it, and for all who would accept his great offer there is freedom from unconscious or mechanical guilt. If a mother shuts her child into a dark closet to discipline it, thinking that she is do-ing right, how does she know that the shock of the closeness and the darkness causes arrested brain development in the child, and, under the action of natural law, he can never rise to his proper intelli-gence? Jesus offered to take her guilt and the child's bearing of the consequences of the same, into his own self, and thereby lift from both mother and child the weight of the law. "God sent forth his son to redeem them that were under the law" *(Gal. 4:5)*. He offered to do this for all unwitting sinners upon the earth. "He is the propitiation for our sins, and not for ours only but also for the sins of the whole world," said John *(I John 2:2)*.

Philip preached this great doctrine to the eunuch *(Acts 8)*. The eunuch asked if possibly it might not be each man's soul taking the consequences of his own unconscious guiltiness. Then Philip preached the opus of Jesus. Let us acknowledge the great and unprecedented and uncopyable achievement of Jesus of Nazareth, who, by recognition of his own Soul, did the humanly impossible. He is the pivotal man. He is the Soul-bloom in the garden of man, the first fruits of them that slept *(I Cor. 15:20)*.

The stillness of our nonrecognition is called sleep. "It is high time that we awake out of sleep," said Paul to the Romans.

We will take Friday to acknowledge before High God the surpassing accomplishment of Jesus of Nazareth. "When thou shalt make his soul the offering for sin, the pleasure of the Lord shall prosper" *(Is. 58)*.

The fifty-third chapter of Isaiah contains the full text of his coming accomplishment. Peter, John, Paul and Philip reaffirm the report as contemporary witnesses of the finished fact. Every one of them tells us to acknowledge before God that we walk through a redeemed healed, unpunishable world, because of the vicarious suffering of Jesus of Nazareth, who, being all Godhood, was and is forever, Christ Jesus — or God Jesus — the living manifestation of what man can do and be by recognition of his own sonship to Omnipotence. "That God the Father may give you the spirit of Wisdom and revelation for the acknowledgment of him" *(Eph. 1:17, margin)*.

He found that death is the result of mechanical or mathematical guiltiness. And he took unto himself death, that might deliver them who through the fear — or expectation — of death were all their lifetime drawn toward death *(Heb. 2:15)*. "He hath abolished death," said Paul *(2 Tim. 1:10)*.

Let us accept our liberty. Let us accept our health, let us accept our redemption, by stating what hath been done. So shall we by sighting one completed work enter upon our own ordained opus. "God is not unrighteous that he will forget our work" *(Heb. 6)*.

As there is but one unit *one,* but as many expressions of the unit one as we please, each occupying an independent and differentiated position, so there is but one Supreme Self in the universe, manifesting as the Self of Jesus, or your self, or myself.

And there is one work for each of us. As Jesus did his work, so we are to do our work. His work was to show the law of vicarious suffering. It is the natural religion of natural man having in it an action not much recognized on earth. The Hindu native women gash their flesh to draw the sufferings of their children to themselves. Catherine of Siena took several sicknesses into herself, and her neighbors were relieved.

We will accept the Scriptural doctrine that "Himself took our infirmities, and bare our sicknesses" (that we might go free) *(Matt. 8)*. We will believe the report, and to us shall the "Arm of the Lord," the finished work of Christ, "be revealed" *(Is. 53)*.

Every, Friday, let us lift up our voices to acknowledge,

"Jesus Christ as Emmanuel (which being interpreted is, God with us), hath borne my griefs and carried my sorrows. He was wounded for my transgressions. He was bruised for my iniquities, the chastisement of my peace was upon him, and by his stripes I am healed. Himself took my infirmities and bare my sicknesses. He is the propitiation for my sins and not for mine only but for the sins of the world."

This acknowledgment is promised to send an ether balm across the heart and brain.

TO REMEMBER:

Commit to memory this page of Bible texts on the sixth Study:

"In him was life; and the life was the light of men." ~ *John 1:4.*

"All things are delivered unto me of my Father." ~ *Matthew 11:27.*

"And whatsoever ye shall ask in my name, that will I do." ~ *John 14:13.*

"That whatsoever ye shall ask of the Father in my name, he may give it you " ~ *John 15:16.*

"I press toward the mark for the prize of the high calling of God in Christ Jesus -- if in anything ye be otherwise minded God shall reveal, even this unto you." ~ *Paul to the Philippians 3:14, 15.*

"Call unto me, and I will answer thee, and show thee great and mighty things which thou knowest not " ~ *Jeremiah 33:3.*

"The Holy Ghost, whom the Father will send in my name, shall teach you all things." ~ *John 14:26.*

VI

ILLUMINATION - UNDERSTANDING[6]

When the disciples had associated with the Risen Christ long enough to sense that he had been wounded for the transgressions of a world, and that by acknowledgment of the same the world might go free -- "then opened he their understanding that they might understand the Scriptures" *(Luke 24:25)*. And the "Scriptures" he gave them was his own name: "The Holy Ghost whom the Father will send in my name shall teach you all things" *(John 14:26)*.

This name constitutes the most remarkable book ever mentioned on earth, for the Spirit of Truth it wakens shall guide into all truth, and show mankind of things to come *(John 16:13)*.

Every man's name conveys his qualities. If he is a strong intellect, the repetition of his name, especially the calling of his name earnestly, imbues

---

[6] This is Saturday morning's study. In later versions letter writing is assigned to Sundays.

the caller with new intellectual strength. If he is heroic in battle, a certain accession of heroism stirs the caller. Cruden, in his immortal Concordance, under the head of "Call," declares that things which had no existence may come into sight by strong words of calling, as *Rom. 4:17*:

> "I have made thee like unto Him, even God, who quickeneth the dead, and calleth those things which be not as though they were." And, "Who hath God so nigh unto them as the Lord our God is in all things that we call unto Him for?" *(Deut. 4:7)*.

Isaiah lamented that no man called for justice *(Is. 59:4)*.

The Gnostics of old proclaimed that the word *Abraxas* was a sacred *pleroma*-name, or word: that is, a sacred word full of blessings, to fall upon whomsoever strongly called it. The Hebrews at one time believed that the fullness of blessing was in the name "Habrakah." Thomas Carlyle called, "O Fortune! Grant me literary distinction!" The giving-forth power of some names has been known for centuries. Canon Farrar, in his *Life of Christ*, says it would be well for us if we were to pick up that old well-known law and practice it.

Surely, by this law, the man who has shown the most superhuman power must confer the most superhuman powers through his name. Therefore the disciples of Jesus Christ became the most wonderful Apostles of doctrine that the world has ever known; for no man's name ever named stands for such colossal achievements as the Christ Jesus they spent so many weeks calling upon.

John the Revelator had been among these callers, and he knew that the little book in the right hand of him that sat upon the throne *(Rev. 5)* was the name, *Jesus Christ.*

"The throne had six steps" (*1 Kings 10:19*). "Six" is the number of attainment to spiritual insight, or illumination above the brain. It is often rendered "understanding." We can know a great deal, be mathematicians, linguists, dialecticians, without this brightness of the Over-Soul shining upon our words and deeds. Man can be so full of mathematics that other men will round the globe to sit at his feet for instruction. This is the meaning of "six"–*i.e.,* throneship.

Man can be so full of epidemic that whosoever, but touches the hem of his garment may be cast down into a bed of sickness. Has anyone seen a man so full of the contagion of God that whosoever touched his raiment was instantly healed, and himself shed abroad health like a contagion?

Saul was told to call upon the name Jesus Christ *(Acts 22).* His name was changed to "Paul", and his aprons and handkerchiefs were full of the contagion of God *(Acts 19).* As many as touched Jesus were made whole *(Matt. 14:36).* Whoever stepped into the shadow of Peter, calling on Jesus Christ, was healed *(Acts 5:15).*

Whosoever called on Minerva the goddess of wisdom, was, in the days of Aristides, the Minerva-imbued Archon of Athens, believed to inhale wisdom.

There was a contagion ready to burst forth in the name of Jesus Christ in old days. That contagion still exists, but there is either curiosity mixed with doubt, or pure doubt without curiosity, in the minds of all who are now told to call upon it, to cry sharply upon it, as Clovis, King of the Franks, cried at the battle of Tolbiac, through and above his doubt, to answering victory.

The name is like an alabaster box that has to be sharply broken open in order that the precious ointment may be obtained. Is it not written, "Thy name is as ointment poured forth?" *(Cant. 1:3)* Nebuchadnezzar called Shadrach, Meshach and Abednego to come forth, and they came forth out of the fiery furnace *(Dan. 3).* Aristides at one time called both Minerva and Aesculapius so sharply and inhaled their influence so thoroughly that they came from the skies and stood plainly in his room.

We will choose the name of the one who wrought forth power over earth and heaven, and in whose name is folded the new name with new powers in it *(Rev. 2:17).* We will choose the name of him who hath redeemed us out of every nation *(Rev. 5).* To sight toward an object and call its name is to finally be related to it. Pope Sixtus V stretched out his hands toward Rome when he was a mere lad and said, "I will be pope of Rome." Then every event and circumstance moved him to the papal seat.

"We can always see how the ideal of a man started with some fixed attention. Abbot Lawrence Lowell, President of Harvard University, had all his life studied principles of government. His steady attention thereto placed him at the head of the College of Governors. We must give our strict attention to something supernally worthwhile. Let us take Saturday and Sunday to call upon the name *Jesus Christ*. As the Jews gathered the same portion of manna for Saturday and Sunday so we will gather the manna promised to fall in the calling of that name *(Rev. 2)*.

"It is the name above every name," said Paul *(Eph. 1)*.

We will stretch our hands and cry to that name. "Doth not Wisdom cry?" *(Prov. 8)*. Let us declare our great need, for he answers, "What wilt thou?" And he has promised, "Whatsoever ye shall ask in my name, that will I do" *(John 14:13)*.

The Zoroastrians believed that the *Ardai Viraf* name reveals the mystic doctrine. Pythagoras believed that there is an ineffable name that is key to the mysteries of the universe. According to the Christian Scriptures the name Jesus Christ is that revealing name, key to all understanding.

TO REMEMBER:

Commit to memory this page of Bible texts on the seventh Study:

"But in the days of the voice of the seventh angel, when he shall begin to sound, the mystery of God should be finished.

"And the voice which I heard from heaven spake unto me again and said, Go and take the little book which is open in the hand of the angel. . . .

"And I took the little book out of the angel's hand, and ate it up, and it was in my mouth sweet as honey: and as soon as I had eaten it my belly was bitter" (mind cure or wormwood).

"And he said unto me, Thou must prophesy again, before many peoples, and nations, and tongues and kings." ~ *Revelation 10:7-11.*

"And the seventh angel poured out his vial into the air; and there came a great voice out of the temple of heaven, from the throne, saying, It is done." ~ *Revelation 16:17.*

"The, tongue of the wise is health." ~ *Proverbs 12:18.*

VII

MINISTRY[7]

And if men slight thee take no heed, And if they hate thee have no care. Sing thou thy song and do thy deed. Hope thou thy hope and pray thy prayer. And claim no crown this does not give. -*Beatty.*

David feels the Spirit of the Lord speaking by him *(2 Sam. 23:2)*. He has caught the tongue of praise. To speak silently the spiritual truth to our neighbor and never to agree with his physical descriptions, is to live by the word of the Spirit, or the Soul's law. It is speaking the truth. "Let every man speak truth to his neighbor, and let none of you imagine evil against him," was the great doctrine of Zechariah *(8:16, 17)*.

It is the day of the new tongue when the true description is perpetually in our heart, and in our thought, and in our speech. This new tongue toward our neighbor is the new preaching, or the new prophesying, which John heard the angel

---

[7] This is Monday midday's study.

telling him to go forth with to the people and to the nations *(Rev. 10)*.

Always "seven" is identified with heavenly speech, or description of the free Spirit. "And when he had opened the seventh seal there was silence in heaven" *(Rev. 8)*. "Heaven" means harmony. "In the seventh place the Lord imparted them speech" *(Apocrypha)*.

To see the free Self is to speak words that harmonize with it. "Beautiful, Strong, Joyous, Flawless," we say silently. We have come to the seventh stone of character, when we see the beautiful, the strong, the flawless namely, the chrysolite stone *(Rev. 21)*. Chrysolite means, "touch of gold."

Nobody is poor or old or sick who comes near the man of right speech; for his tongue is health whether he speaks silently or audibly *(Prov. 12: 18)*. Pliny wrote that some people carry health by their presence. No one can fail to carry health if his secret tongue is all praise, never yielding to condemnation, no matter what the claim or temptation.

"At the seventh hour Jesus said, 'Go thy way, thy son liveth'" *(John 4)*. It is the seventh praise repeated over and over that the Seventh Angel starts. Joshua sounded the horns over and over on the seventh day.

All the rest of our life we are to praise the free Self of our neighbor. No man so mistaken, but we are to praise his wise free Spirit only. No man so negligent or reprehensible, but we are to praise silently his integrity and righteousness. No man so old, but we are to praise his beautiful free Self. No man so sick or lame, but we are to praise his flawless divinity.

On Monday we must choose some sick or palsied or wicked person, as he appears outwardly, and praise his divine Self. Speak silently to his Omnipotent God-self. No matter how long it takes, keep on, Monday, after Monday.

"The Lord turned the captivity of Job when he prayed for his friends" *(Job 42:10).* Something falls away from us as we pray in the words of praise and command to the Free Omnipotence, or the Jesus Christ of our Neighbor.

Pantaleon, in days of Maximian, took a palsied and dying man by the hand and spoke to his Jesus Christ free Self, and the man was instantly healed.

There is no set formula for praising the transcending Self. Joseph kept on sighting peace and silently speaking peace to his eleven brethren, exactly as his father Jacob had commanded him, for twenty years. At last the brethren were all healed, even of wickedness.

Here is a silent description with great awakening in it. Make it the key speech or your opinion of your neighbor every time you see him outwardly as sick, or poor or unhappy. Let no such images keep before your eye. Remember the Real Self. Describe it. And on Monday remember the particular case you are to bring forth out of the darkness, as:

I see you, John Marston, above, transcending your past. I see you unweighted, free; I see you as complete Spirit. Nothing can be added to you; nothing can be taken from you. I see you as Health. You are one with Universal Health. Nothing can spoil Universal Health. It is God putting away disease. I see you as Omnipotence. Nothing can defeat Omnipotence. It puts aside weakness and shows me God working before me for you, and through you, and by you, forever and ever. You face me up as God, unweighted, unattached, unspoiled forever and ever. I see you as Wisdom looking toward me to speak by you of your heavenly wholeness and peace. I *see* you as Peace. I see you facing me as Peace that the world cannot take away. I see you as Peace putting aside discord. God is showing Peace now with its touch on your outer life at every point. You are free God becoming visible for my sake, that truth may prevail.

By the grace of God Almighty—the grace of the Holy Ghost—by the grace of Jesus Christ now falling upon you and working in you, I command you to show yourself to all the world as untainted Health and free Omnipotence from this day forth.

NOTES

What are you looking — when you see people
look above them for the soul

K: Jake what would Jesus do — take the class
when back in the world
what comes up

I will
often   not accuse. but look for their
soul.

I might be thinking — I can look alone
when I listen

Assumption — I will be in the world
& make a difference in it

TO REMEMBER:

Commit to memory this page of Bible texts on the eighth Study:

"Circumcised on the eighth day." ~ *Philippians 3:5.*

"Ye stiff-necked and uncircumcised in heart and ears, ye do always resist the Holy Ghost: as your fathers did, so *do ye.*" ~ *Acts 7:51.*

"He that escapeth shall come unto thee to cause thee to hear it with thine ears." ~ *Ezekiel 24:26.*

"The ears, of them that hear shall hearken." ~ *Isaiah 32:3.*

"For through the voice of the Lord shall the Assyrian be beaten down…" ~ *Isaiah 30:81*

"Thine ears shall hear a word behind thee saying, this is the way." ~ *Isaiah 30:21.*

"The accuser of our brethren is cast down." ~ *Revelation 12:10.*

"Every tongue that shall rise against thee in judgment, thou shalt condemn." ~ *Isaiah 54:17.*

"Now go, write it before them in a book." ~ *Isaiah 30:8.*

"Blotting out the handwriting of ordinances against us nailing it to his cross…" ~ *Colossians 2:14.*

"The eighth, a beryl…" ~ *Revelation 21:20.*

"The eighth was Shimeon" (hearkening) ~ *Ezra 10:31.*

VIII

MINISTRY[8]

"The eighth lot came forth to Abijah" *(1 Chron. 24).* "Abijah" is the son of the speaker, Aaron. A "son" is an idea. The order is very direct. An idea always comes to us at some point in our description of the Real Self of our neighbor. This idea tells us what to add to our previous phrases and commands. Each neighbor needs some special message. When an idea comes we can speak it audibly to the neighbor, if we like. Its effect is almost always instantaneous. If it is the message his whole being craves, his disease will soon drop off and his smile break forth.

King Bruce watched a spider, and a sudden courage and valor flamed up in him. He had stopped his own thinking for a few seconds, and what he watched affected his whole constitution. St. Cyran, Father Confessor at the Port Royal Nunnery, instructed the nuns to look toward God in a listening attitude. "He has something to tell you," said St. Cyran.

---

[8] This is Tuesday midday's study

In the Talmud it is written that the Messiah will come when the people hearken to the voice of God. In the Old Testament, we are told that the escaped or the free Spirit, will cause us to hear, or to have the right idea *(Ez. 24:26)*. After eight days, Jesus the Risen came visibly present to the waiting disciples, and said, "Peace be unto you." *(John 20)*.

Peter and James and John heard Moses and Elias speaking of the future of Jesus, after about eight days *(Luke 9)*. Aeneas had kept his bed eight years waiting for the right word, which Peter then gave him *(Acts 9:33)*.

There is the word of punishment if the eye is downward toward the sinfulness of the people. Ezekiel was a great hearkener for the punishments that are exactly meted out to different sins. So did the Zoroastrians hearken for the different kinds of results of different wickednesses: "If crime is not punished, there shall be pestilence." "If justice is not done to the innocent, war shall follow." "When some pay tithes, and some do not, drought is the punishment."

It is only the upward watcher who hears the promise of peace and health and forgiveness. Ben Soma, the Jew, hears the words, "Despise no person and no thing for everyone and each thing have their appointed hour." That which is told from above is always of universal application and universal worth and is therefore worth writing, as we have been taught by Jeremiah *(30:2)*, "Write thee all the words that I have spoken unto thee in a book."

We may spend a while in a listening attitude before one whose Free Omnipotence we have praised. The air has been spiritualized by describing silently the Free Spirit. We are ready, like Hannah *(1 Sam.)*, to hear the words which strike into view the answer to our prayer. "He shall come unto thee to cause thee to hear" *(Ez. 24)*.

We must repeat the idea firmly, as if it were the final word. Zechariah repeated it three times: "Thus saith the Lord of hosts, Turn ye unto me" *(Zech. 1)*.

The "eighth" is circumcision *(Phil. 3:5)*. "Circumcised on the eighth day" means that we are cut off from the stories of pain, disease, poverty, death. We are hearkening intently to the heavenly speech. "O ye uncircumcised of heart and of ear!" cried Stephen, "Ye do always resist the Holy Ghost" *(Acts 7)*. The Holy Ghost is the teacher. The harvest of sayings from the Holy Ghost above causes the end of the world *(Matt. 13)*.

The sign of the cross is the sign of the undoing of the past by the sight and hearing of the New. It is the sign of the blotting out of ordinances against us, as Paul discovered *(Col 2)*. The Egyptians and the Chaldeans made the sign of the cross to signify that the present state of affairs is blotted out. The priests of Isis blotted out the evil. The priests of Serapis blotted out the good, "I can make wiles in battle; I can make corn and cattle; that they shall never thrive," was their chant.

The Christian St. Felix spat upon the metal image of Serapis in the time of Diocletian, and it fell down from its pedestal and was literally broken to powder. Spittle was in old times regarded as a charm by Jews, Greeks and Romans. When they made the sign of the cross they wet the finger with spittle. It is the symbol of erasure.

As soon as Odilo of Cluny met sickness or blindness he wet his finger and made the sign of the cross, to signify that what was presenting itself was nothing at all: the unseen Christ was all.

How can the ears hear the truth regarding a blind man while the blindness seems so real and sad? No wonder that we need to have some sign that the flesh profiteth nothing, as Jesus said *(John 6)*. Only the words of the Healing Spirit are life and healing strength.

Take Tuesday to blot out all the words of sickness, pain and death. Take Tuesday to erase the pain, poverty and disease, from over the free Spirit of some one person. Take Tuesday to hearken to the particular message that belongs to Monday's case. Hearken all day Tuesday to the voice of the Lord whispering behind thee, as Isaiah said *(Isaiah 30)*. It comes as an idea. It is undeniably true. Remember that the truth makes free *(John 8)*.

All sick, or lame, or unhappy people would spring suddenly into freedom if some one would speak to them the truth belonging to them. "A right word, how good it is; who can measure the force of a right word?" "He sent forth his word and healed them" *(Ps. 107:20).* "He wakeneth thine ear to hear as the learned" *(Is. 50:4).* "The tongue of the wise is health" *(Prov. 12:18).* "A good word maketh the heart glad" *(Prov. 12:25).* "The Lord God hath opened mine ear and I was not rebellious, neither turned away back" *(Is. 50:5).*

They that can hear the word of healing have touched the beryl stone of character. They are of value on land and sea as the beryl stone is the color of both land and sea. Their written words convey health to all who read them.

TO REMEMBER:

Commit to memory this page of Bible texts on the ninth Study:

"The ninth a topaz." ~ *Revelation 21:20,*

"The topaz was in the breastplate, and had the name of Simeon upon it." ~ Cruden's *Concordance, p. 687.*

"Thy words were found and I did eat them, and thy word was unto me the joy and rejoicing of my heart." ~ *Jeremiah 15:16.*

"The joy of the Lord is your strength." ~ *Nehemiah 8:10.*

"The friend of the bridegroom, which standeth and heareth, rejoiceth greatly." ~ *John 3:29.*

"He that is of a merry heart hath a continual feast." ~ *Proverbs 16:15.*

"A merry heart doeth good like a medicine." ~ *Proverbs 17:22*

"They shall lay hands on the sick, and they shall recover." ~ *Mark 16:18.*

"Ye shall eat of old fruit till the ninth year." ~ *Leviticus 25:22.*

IX

MINISTRY[9]

The law of listening is the law of joy. "The friend of the bridegroom, which standeth and heareth, rejoiceth greatly" *(John 3:29).* The upward watcher gets his inner ear opened to know how matters and things are progressing.

Isaiah tells Hezekiah: "Thou shalt die." He is judging by the law of impetus downward. He does not see that Hezekiah has obeyed his prophets' injunction to lift up his eyes and behold who is the Creator *(Is. 40:26).* King Hezekiah had a strong moral vitality and could lift up his eyes out of the depths of pain and death, and proclaim with all his heart, that the upward watch was life, even though his eyes were failing *(Is. 38).*

Isaiah did not have very cheerful views of his neighbors. This was the rock on which he split.

The mystics have always failed in proportion as they have insisted on the wickedness and failings of their neighbors. Even Zechariah, who

---

[9] This is Wednesday midday's study

proclaimed that we must never imagine evil of or against anybody, was so under the spell of the prophets before him that he heard the voice of the howling of the wicked shepherds *(Zech. 11:3)*, and not the chants of the forgiven.

But even at the cross Jesus saw the forgiven world. It is a matter of strong fixed sight that gives the ideas that show in conduct and flesh.

If you forget a name look steadily toward the person who bears it and the name will come to you. If you do not get it promptly it is evident that your vision does not stay fixed. The photographic plate has to be exposed to the object long enough to catch its impress distinctly or the configuration is indistinct. Try again and look longer. Looking toward God on high, Moses caught laws just suited to people of his age. Looking toward God on high, Mohammed caught laws just suited to people of his age. Looking toward God on high we can catch the law just suited to the person who seems to be unhappy. If we do not catch the law at first we must look again.

The words caught from above have always uplifting and healing potency in them. "Thy word was unto me the joy and rejoicing of my heart" *(Jer. 15:16)*.

The description of the strong and beautiful Self localizes the universal truth. This localizing is called healing. "I will give you pastors that shall feed you with knowledge," said the Lord to Jeremiah, (Jer. 3), and all the people shall be new and glad. How can pastors feed with the joy of right if they have not themselves been fed?

The Hindus have taught that we must animate the particular from the universal. The "Particular" is the man or object. There is a root of strength and vitality about everybody and everything that the right speech with the right tonic in it would animate into astonishing virility. Even an apparently dead tree is reachable by one with this mystery of vitalizing tone in his secret speech.

It is an unkillable quality resident at the roots of life, as the actinic ray that sweetens the grape is an unquenchable constituent of the sunshine.

Joy must be quickened from somewhere. The Scriptures declare that it is quickened from hearing vitalizing truth. "Thy words were found and I did eat them; and thy word was unto me the joy and rejoicing of my heart" (Jer. 15: 16).

This joy that comes of being in direct communication with the I AM is an increasable product. Gideon got such a new estimate of himself by coming into speaking relationship with the Supernal Original, that he rose from being of no consequence among the Jews to bold leadership. Abraham talked with angels, and transcended his neighbors.

We speak to the Soul, the Jesus Christ of man, and we are comrading with the Supernal neighbor.

We are keeping high company. God hath set us on high because we have first known his name *(Ps. 91:14)*, and at every turn we behold Divinity manifesting as beauty, health, joy, the outward signs of the Universal Highest. Joy is the leviathan power resident in man. Whoever can wake God joy in his neighbor brings forth the most powerful principle he covers.

It is a secret charm which people covet and follow after and get comfort from. Haggai says that it is the real desire of all nations *(Hag. 2:7)*. He is told three times in the ninth month that the heavens shall shake and the desire of the nations shall come *(Hag. 2)*. Its symbol is the topaz stone. The true topaz is so valuable that it is worth a million dollars. It signifies that the triumph of steadfast vision has come in the words which set nobility where wickedness had hitherto been visible, as Joseph's long vision and unvarying speech, under the direction of his father Jacob *(Gen. 37)*, finally transformed his murderous brethren into lovers; as Peter and John transformed the impotent man at the gate of the Temple called Beautiful *(Acts 3)*, and in these days certain people among us can transform cramps and deformity into beauty.

Ofttime glancing to the Heights brings back transforming words that stir the joy chords. For it is a joy to tell the words that transform pain into peace, and disease into health. It awakens youth to feel the joy currents leap within us. It makes the hand magnetic to the angel, so that it pulls the angel of man's presence forward when we stretch forth the hand.

Jesus touched the free Spirit of the leper *(Matt. 8)*, and the angel of the child of Nain *(Luke 7)*. He said we ought to lay hands on the sick to make them recover *(Mark 10:18)*.

He means that we have come to the ninth stone of character, where the angel is tangible to us. The early Roman Catholics called the tangibility of the angels the real meaning of the number nine.

Let us practice touching the invisible yet tangibly present angel of some sick person. Let us take Wednesday to stretch forth invisible bands and urge the angel to make himself manifest. This urge is our will. It is the man's will. It is God's will. This is the song of the topaz, viz., the universal will to be well.

There is a pulling power in the hand as we say to the Angel of the presence, "Come forth! It is God's will, it is your will, it is my will that you be well and strong and glad. Come forth!" Tell him your most joyous text. Repeat it over and over as a song is "I drew them with cords, with bands of love — and they knew not that I healed them" *(Hosea 11:4, 3)*.

TO REMEMBER:

Commit to memory this page of Bible texts on the tenth Study:

"The tenth shall be holy to the Lord." ~ *Leviticus 27:32.*

"And the people blessed all the men that willingly offered themselves to dwell in Jerusalem." ~ *Nehemiah 11:1, 2.*

"And the people came up out of Jordan on the tenth day." ~ *Joshua, 4:19.*

"Then shalt thou cause the trumpet of the jubilee to sound on the tenth day." ~ *Leviticus 25:9.*

"I will put my law in their inward parts." ~ *Jeremiah 31:33.*

"They said unto him, Master, where dwellest thou? He saith unto them, 'Come and see.' They came and saw where he dwelt, and abode with him that day, for it was about the tenth hour." ~ *John 1:38, 39.*

"I in you…" ~ *John 14:20.*

"Go stand and speak to the people in the temple." ~ *Acts 5:20.*

X

MINISTRY[10]

Confidence,
confident 3rd
?
?

The tenth stone of character is the chrysopra-sus *(Rev. 21)*. This signifies that no situation daunts us. The people came up out of the raging waters of Jordan on the tenth day *(Josh. 4)*, but they had not noticed the raging waters, their vision was so glued to liberty. To them the water had parted *(Josh. 3)*.

When we mean to heal our neighbor we some-times find that his whole secret mind opposes the healing truth we so ardently tell him. His mind and body get excited with pain or sickness. All his old diseases show forth. Dysentery, influ-enza, fever, rheumatism, disturb him. He is irrita-ble, confused, weepy.

To be phased by such a showing forth is to prove that we have not come to the tenth stone of character.   "If thou faint in the day of adversity, thy strength is small," said Solomon *(Prov. 24:10)*.

---

[10] This is Thursday midday's study

To stand on our stone of confidence, assurance, certainty, with respect to a man who is very sick, is to reach the everlasting health which shines like a sun back of his sickness. That sun with its healing beams can brush aside his sickness as the sun in the skies brushes aside the clouds. The clouds may hurry and scurry and glower darkly, but they have nothing to do with altering the sun. The sun is the same it was before the clouds gathered.

When the Sun of health back of sickness is once seen, the sickness is not recognized. It is a great day when nothing moves us, either pain, or disease, or crying, because we are sighting the reality of peace. It brings forth a happy neighbor. He feels the apple green of a new base. He suddenly shines forth saying, "I see that my life is God, to whom I am looking for life."

After years of looking upward to God as his Sovereign, a man, passing through many vicissitudes, was suddenly set into prosperity beyond his expectations. This gave him great leverage with his neighbors, and his doctrine that "God reigns," was hastened to. He was not looking for money; he was looking for the Great Fiat, "Look unto me," and the Divine Providence, the Countenance that shineth was his goal, but the effect was a dominant relationship with his fellow men.

The adversities that shrouded his path had been the opposing activities that would have shrouded through his whole lifetime had not his high statement and his high watch held out to the end, finally parting the waters of his Jordan.

To yield to doubt and fear because conditions are gloomy is not to hold out to the end of the clouds. Some people let go of God and the great truth that they started forth with. So they never see their victory in this life. It is pretty certain they will have to try again somewhere, but how much better to settle the question of the high watch and the truth of the Soul right here, now!

Our neighbor is Free Spirit. No pain, no disease, can be added to the free Spirit, or taken from it. Our neighbor is not flesh and blood, quaking and crying. We touch him as the angel of God's presence. We speak to him as Omnipotent Soul. This is truth, whether he shows it outwardly today or not. If he does not show it outwardly, but instead he complains and has more trouble than ever, the truth is true all the same.

"Mine integrity within me," said David *(Ps. 1:8)*. Job's wife asked him if he still held to his integrity while he was still in his misery *(Job 2:9)*.

At our interior God-point we see as God sees and know as God knows. In the midst of affliction we must speak forth this secret knowing and seeing. It is the heavenly fact told us in secret to be proclaimed upon the housetops *(Matt. 10)*.

Whenever anyone to whom we have whispered the praises of Soul begins to act quite wretched in his body, let us look to our temple place, our sanctuary within, where we know as God and see as God. Let us "look to the rock whence we are hewn" *(Is. 51)*. Let us read from the law as it is in our inward parts *(Jer. 31:33)*.

We will take Thursday to regard our neighbor as within, at our hidden meeting place with God. Also on Thursday we will speak to the one that we love best, at our meeting place with God.

> In mine integrity within me, where I see as God and know as God, I know you, John Child, as free Spirit. I know you as alive with life that death cannot touch. I know you as strong with Omnipotence, whole and complete as Son of God, wise to know yourself as unhurt by matter or mind. Show yourself to all the world as I know you at my integrity point. Acknowledge with boldness and confidence that you are free, strong, glad Spirit, without pain or disease.

This is a good treatment to give concerning one who has had an accident or who has been taken suddenly ill. It takes him past the chemical change, or Jordan River he is passing through. There was an angel near Daniel when he fainted and was sick certain days.

There is an angel always standing near one in trouble. Let us agree with the angel and see health and strength made visible by our firm secret insistence.

"He hath put wisdom in the inward parts" *(Job 38:36)*. There is no healing that we can trust like the healing that comes from recognizing from own unshakable centre just how it is forever with our neighbor.

"Go stand and speak to the people in the temple," said the angel to the apostles *(Acts 5:20)*.

"Ye are the temple" *(I Cor. 3)*. "I in you" *(John 14:20)*.

This practice disciplines for new and impromptu treatments unsuggested by previous experiences. "Now therefore go, and I will be with thy mouth, and teach thee what thou shalt say" *(Ex. 4:12)*.

TO REMEMBER:

Commit to memory this page of Bible texts on the eleventh Study:

"And they took knowledge of them that they had been with Jesus." ~ *Acts 4:13.*

"Thou hast been in Eden, the Garden of God; and the ruby was thy covering." ~ *Ezekiel 28.*

"My judgment was unto me a robe." ~ *Job 29:14.*

"A king that sitteth in the throne of judgment, scattereth away all evil with his eyes." ~ *Proverbs 20:8.*

"God is judge himself." ~ *Psalm 50:6.*

"Their judgment shall proceed of themselves." ~ *Habakkuk 1:7.*

"I will make my judgment to rest for a light." ~ *Isaiah 51:4.*

"All the heathen shall see my judgment." ~ *Ezekiel 39:21.*

"In the eleventh year was the house finished." ~ *I Kings 6:38.*

XI

MINISTRY[11] *judgment*

"In the eleventh year was the house finished," and Solomon said that whosoever should look to the house would be set at liberty (*I Kings 6*).

"House" signifies character. A man's judgment constitutes the sum total of his character. A good judge is more sought unto than a king, for he establishes right relations, man with man. Something about right appeals. Even an infant weeps at injustice and stops weeping when justice is rendered.

One with right judgment according to the Jesus Christ of himself knows instantly what to do to heal the sick man, or raise the dead man, or help the disheartened.

All the voluntary practices of the presence of God which we are making have been the inspirations of such as have beheld their Heavenly Father's countenance till they knew that whatever they themselves did was right, and they could see that

---

[11] This is Friday midday's study

65

whatever was happening outwardly had back of it and over it some wonderful blessing. They did not have to scramble and pull things and events into order. By sighting the Trend, or the Providence, or the Fiat, and seeing the finished fact, they accomplished mighty things.

St. John of the Cross ploughed twice as many furrows as any other of the monks, because his eye was on the finished land of God. The whole creation is finished, complete, now, in the eyes of God. To see for three seconds a thing in its completeness, as it truly is, is to find the thing acting of its own weight to exhibit itself to everybody as complete.

Dr. Gordon of Boston wrote about the new healing as a process of seeing a strong arm where a withered one claimed to exist, as Jesus cried with a loud voice to the living Lazarus.

Whatever we see with the inner eye comes by and by to the outer eye. Everywhere we look a finished objective faces us. It is the thing as God sees it. "Why dost thou show me iniquity?" cried Habakkuk, "therefore doth judgment never go forth from me" (*Hab. 1*). It is the angel of repose between God and man to see as God sees. "Is he not too pure to behold iniquity?" (*Hab. 1:13*).

The Mohammedan Caliph Ali found that every man's lot or portion in life is seeking him, or looking toward him. He called upon us to be at rest from seeking our good. It is in straight line with us. We can pray as if we had received, for here it is, no matter what it is we have asked for. "Pray as if ye had received ~ believe that ye receive," said Jesus *(Mark 11)*. "Ask what ye will," he said *(John 15)*.

Judgment is communicable. Rai Shalligram, a postmaster in Northwestern India, saw that Divine Providence was under his feet and moving along with him. It was so real to him that he concluded to go away from his good business and let himself be fed without doing anything at all. Providence would always take good care of him, he said. No one could look at the light burning in the upper chamber of his house without feeling that he also could give up his business and be a wanderer, fed by Universal Good.

Notice how the mothers of India threw their babies into the Ganges, because their dervishes held the fixed judgment that it was pleasing to God to drown infants. Notice how the Shunammite woman said her child was well, because she saw Elisha's face, and his judgment laid its steadying words of life on her heart *(2 Kings 4)*.

So we catch God-judgment from the face of God. "Many seek the ruler's face, but every man's judgment cometh from the Lord," said Solomon *(Prov. 29:26)*. We have generally caught only prejudices, notions, what Jeremiah called "foxes across Mount Zion" *(Lam. 5)*.

We will take Friday to stop throwing any estimates out over people. We will let the finished good of them declare itself to us.

By this stopping of thoughts engendered by associating with downward watching men, the Son of God faces us in all men, and his judgment and our judgment is one judgment.

"The eleven stars did obeisance to Joseph" *(Gen. 37)*. This means that every estimate falls down into nothingness before the God-estimate. "Joseph" means, "he will add." That is, he will add to life as it now stands, a life by a miracle of God. He will add to gold as it now stands riches by the miracle of God.

Joab told David not to count his army. "God shall add unto the people an hundred-fold how many soever they may be," he said. But David's own judgment was hot within him, and Joab's words were unheeded. So there was disaster in Jerusalem *(2 Sam. 24)*.

To let the ark move forward is to let the great Trend alone, to rest, because it is finished. "In earing time and harvest thou shalt rest," for, "God shall bring forth thy judgment as the noon-day" *(Ps. 37:6)*.

"The eleventh was the jacinth" — the red rubelite. Pushing red to its acme of perfection it is the priceless ruby, emblem of priceless judgment.

Beauty is another word for judgment. Beauty is poise, balance, as judgment is balance. "Out of Zion, the perfection of beauty, God hath shined" (*Ps. 50:2*).

According to Thy judgment it is well with me, therefore it is well.   According to Thy judgment it is well with all men, therefore it is well.

TO REMEMBER:

Commit to memory this page of Bible texts on the twelfth Study:

"And the twelfth lot came forth to Jakim" (whom God sets up). ~ *I Chronicles 24:12.*

"And the twelfth lot came forth to Hashabiah" (leader of the hosts of song). ~ *I Chronicles 25:19.*

"The twelfth foundation was an amethyst." ~ *Revelations 21:20.*

"Canst thou bring forth the twelve signs" ~ *Job 38:32 (margin).*

"Then two shall be in the field; the one shall be taken, the other left." ~ *Luke 17:36.*

"To the angel of the church in Pergamos, write..." ~ *Revelations 2:12*

To your Angel, Greeting: ~

You are Spirit of Life, making hardy the flesh and inspiring the perceptions ~

You quicken the whole being with genius ~

You fix the heart with divine purpose ~

You write your name with the Saints of Light ~

Your new powers are to-day manifest.

XII

MINISTRY[12] *rest, arrival*
the 'work' has arrived, it is done,

"The twelfth lot came forth to Jakim" - whom God sets up (*I Chron. 24:12*). "He is set on high because he hath known my name" (*Ps. 91:14*). Jakim is head of the twelfth course of priests. Jakim, the true high priest, is not man-taught. He is taught from above. Elisha was such a priest and this put him at the head of the schools of the prophets at Jericho and Gilgal.

He had poured water on the hands of Elijah and otherwise waited upon him like a menial, because he had seen that Elijah communed face to face with Jehovah. This gave a quality to the association. "Where is the God of Elijah?" was his cry when Elijah flew upward (*2 Kings 2:14*). He did not mourn Elijah's departure. His secret quest was God.

Tesla's secret vigils with electricity have set him in the forefront of electricians. Napoleon's secret watch toward high seats gave him the crown.

---

[12] In later versions, Lesson XII is assigned to Saturday midday and letter writing is assigned to Sunday afternoon.

"And the twelfth lot came forth to Hashabiah," head of the twelfth course of Levitical singers (*I Chron. 6*). The Levitical singers cause men to forget trouble and anger as Elisha forgot his animosity toward King Jehoram, when he heard the musical instruments playing dulcet melodies *(2 Kings 3)*, as Paul and Silas forgot they were in prison while singing of the free Spirit *(Acts 16)*.

When curses can be turned into blessings we have touched the divine alchemy. The oyster that turns the anguish-giving sand grain into a pearl with the lustre of the skies in its whiteness, is emblem of man glorying in the midst of affliction. "We glory in tribulations," said Paul *(Rom. 5:3)*. Paul was the collect of all the Apostolic virtues in the earth. It took all the twelve Apostles to strike his curses into blessings. He was the convert from animosity to identification. "Canst thou bring forth the twelve signs?" asks God of Job *(38:32)*.

Any moment our obedient watch may turn Saul into a Paul among those unto whom we are ministering. The practice of looking toward the Judge of all earth who doeth right *(Gen. 18:25)*, causes us to recognize the right judgment native to every man, woman, child, on earth.

As what we recognize comes to the surface in its own good time, our neighbor's outward actions and speech must soon be according to our recognition.

Men catch our prejudices as they catch our measles. They catch our right judgment as they catch our smallpox. Notice how soon our family stops drinking tea if we have a prejudice against tea. Notice how soon they look up if we look up.

"By me kings reign," saith the Lord of Hosts *(Prov. 8:15).* This means that we have kingship by associating with the king. We have wisdom by associating with the Author of Wisdom. "I will instruct thee and teach thee," he saith *(Ps. 32:8).*

At a certain point of attention to mathematics the student touches the origin of reckoning and can perform any given calculation with numbers. Then he is master of his art. He radiates reckoning. It is the same with the musician. Zangwill's Baal Shem was Master of the Holy Name and could work miracles by it. But he had had to give strict attention to it for a lifetime before its magic mysteries were his own. At the point of their radiating mathematics, the Oriental monarchs sought the Masters of the science of mathematics to associate with royal children, that they might easily outstrip other children.

At the point of identification with the King of Kings and Lord of Lords, the world seeks the men and women so identified, to snatch health and vigor from their bright flying sparks of secret God-quality. They rest from their efforts but their works are effectual, as it is written, "They rest from their labors, and their works do follow them" *(Rev. 14:13).*

God gives us this rest, and our works go forth.

"I will give you rest," he saith *(Matt. 11:28).* Did not Paul's clothing radiate his secret relationship with Him who healeth all our diseases?

It is the highest state of ministry possible when without thinking anything or trying in any way to help our neighbors we are yet their health and their joy. "Let us labor therefore to enter into that rest," said Paul *(Heb. 4:11).*

The twelfth symbolic stone of character is the amethyst *(Rev. 21).* It is the emblem of rest, of arrival. The harness is put off; we, passing through the valley of Baca (weeping), make it a well of refreshment *(Ps. 84:6).*

As the ruby is most precious of all the precious stones, so the amethyst is least precious, in the estimation of man. It is the emblem of taking the weak things of this world to confound the mighty and the prudent *(1 Cor. 1:27).* He who touches the twelfth characteristic has no hope. What shall one hope for who hath attained all? Does the bridegroom hope for his bride when she is already the mother of his children? The amethyst symbolizes one without expectation. This is a state held in low esteem on earth, but in heaven it is the state of the angels. He who touches the twelfth characteristic is indifferent to sickness and crying. Does the sun regard whether it is ripening the apple or rotting the pear?

He is the greatest healer who is so identified with Health that even his outer ears cannot hear complaints of sickness. "Who is deaf as my messenger that I sent?" saith the Lord *(Is. 42:19)*. The Lord's messenger sees only the Lord's finished work. He hears only the talk of wholeness. To him there is neither male nor female *(Gal. 8:28)*. To him it is easy to eat what is set before him, and ask no questions *(1 Cor. 10)*.

Paul did not go between them. He did not go on to the language beyond eating and not eating, though he had risen to say that neither if we eat are we the better, nor if we eat not are we the worse *(1 Cor. 8:8)*. We must go on to the next language. We must not stop to discuss what is right or wrong to eat, or what is the difference between the sexes.

The two that are in the field are, Soul unmolested, and flesh in mental turmoil. "Two shall be in the field," said Jesus the Master of the Unspoken Name; "the one shall be taken, the other left" *(Matt. 24:40)*.

John the Revelator told us to write to the Soul, whenever the mind and body present intellect, vanity or emotion, like a church wall of hiding to our doctrine.

There are seven types to whose angel we must write *(Rev. 2)*. First, there is the Ephesus type. They are the emotional, the excitement lovers. Then the Smyrnans. They are the lovers of adornment. Then there are the Pergamites. These are the lovers of art, literature, science and statecraft. Pergamos had temples dedicated to the gods of science, art, and government of life. The one to Science, whose keynote is healing was called *Aesculapius*. Out of the Pergamos type is to come the writer of the little book which is to alter the life of the world and usher in a new dispensation. Then there is the Sardis type. These are body devotees. They are afraid of draughts. They are afraid of what they eat. They are always seeking the comfortable, the soft, the pleasant things of bodily life. Then there are the Thyatirans. These are the easily offended. And the Philadelphians, who are the philanthropists of human existence, who seem so worthwhile yet whose vision is glued to human woe; we must write to their angel, otherwise their mind will never agree with the doctrine of unmolested Sonship to Jehovah. We must write to the angel of the Laodiceans also. These are the people who are always changing their religion.

We need not show these people the letters we have written to them. We can burn the letters. All addresses to the angel have subtle flavors that can penetrate through the strong walls of unlikeness to the meanings, without the necessity for acknowledged communion. Kings shall know that which they have not been taught, said Isaiah, in his fifty-second chapter.

"Now ye are come to an innumerable company of angels, written in heaven," said Paul to the Hebrews.

We must take Saturday and Sunday[13] of each week to write to the angel of some otherwise unreachable neighbor. We must keep high company. We are on a great ministry. It is no less than showing men their Sonship to God and their inheritance of the Jesus Christ character, free from the law of matter.

---

[13] In later versions, Lesson XII is assigned to Saturday midday and letter writing is assigned to Sundays.

NOTES

SUGGESTION

Fill the blank pages with quotations from philosophers, poets, mystics, on the foregoing twelve points.

Put with them your own original inspirations as they come to you. So will you write your name with the stars, and make the foundation of an original book.

It has been prophesied that a little book is to come to the world, altering its life and ushering in a new dispensation.

No station in life, no age, no sex, no color, no previous acquirements, shall indicate the writer of the book.

Only the Keeper of the Name and the High Watch can write it. Should your hand pen the revolutionizing doctrine, no heart so praiseful as mine.

E. C. H.

We are courting spirit
repent – turn away & seek Spirit
we are silent til 5.

NOTES

	am	noon
Monday	1	7
Tues	2	8
Wed	3	9
Thurs	4	10
Fri	5	11
Saturday	6	12

NOTES

NOTES

NOTES

NOTES

Other Books by Emma Curtis Hopkins

- *Class Lessons of 1888 (WiseWoman Press)*
- *Bible Interpretations (WiseWoman Press)*
- *Esoteric Philosophy in Spiritual Science (WiseWoman Press)*
- *Genesis Series 1894 (WiseWoman Press)*
- *High Mysticism (WiseWoman Press)*
- *Self Treatments with Radiant I Am (WiseWoman Press)*
- *The Gospel Series (WiseWoman Press)*
- *Judgment Series in Spiritual Science (WiseWoman Press)*
- *Drops of Gold (WiseWoman Press)*
- *Resume (WiseWoman Press)*
- *Scientific Christian Mental Practice (DeVorss)*

Books about Emma Curtis Hopkins and her teachings

- *Emma Curtis Hopkins, Forgotten Founder of New Thought* – Gail Harley
- *Unveiling Your Hidden Power: Emma Curtis Hopkins' Metaphysics for the 21st Century (also as a Workbook and as A Guide for Teachers)* – Ruth L. Miller
- *Power to Heal: Easy reading biography for all ages* –Ruth Miller

To find more of Emma's work, including some previously un-published material, log on to:

www.emmacurtishopkins.com

WISEWOMAN PRESS

800.603.3005

www.wisewomanpress.com

Books Published by WiseWoman Press

By Emma Curtis Hopkins

- Resume
- High Mysticism
- Class Lessons of 1888
- The Gospel Series
- Self Treatments including Radiant I Am
- Esoteric Philosophy in Spiritual Science
- Judgment Series in Spiritual Science
- Drops of Gold Journal
- Genesis Series 1894
- Bible Interpretations: Series I-XVII

By Ruth L. Miller

- Unveiling Your Hidden Power: Emma Curtis Hopkins' Metaphysics for the 21st Century
- Coming into Freedom: Emily Cady's Lessons in Truth for the 21st Century
- 150 Years of Healing: The Founders and Science of New Thought
- Power Beyond Magic: Ernest Holmes Biography
- Power to Heal: Emma Curtis Hopkins Biography
- The Power of Unity: Charles Fillmore Biography
- The Power of Mind: Phineas P. Quimby Biography
- The Power of Insight: Thomas Troward Biography
- The Power of the Self: Ralph Waldow Emerson Biography
- Uncommon Prayer
- Spiritual Success
- Finding the Path

By Ute Maria Cedilla

- The Mysticism of Emma Curtis Hopkins